© Indica Cards • www.mpu.co.in

indica.cards@gmail.com +91-93124 01976

Birla Temple (Laxmi Narain Temple): Built by Birla's in 1938 A.D. and dedicated to Lord Vishnu and his consort Laxmi, it contains many idols of Hindu sects. The opening ceremony was performed by M. Gandhi.

© Indica Cards • www.mpu.co.in

indica.cards@gmail.com +91-93124 01976

Birla Temple (Laxmi Narayan Temple): Built by Birla's in 1938 A.D. and dedicated to Lord Vishnu and his consort Laxmi, it contains many idols of Hindu sects. The opening ceremony was performed by M. Gandhi.

indica.cards@gmail.com +91-93124 01976

Laxmi Narain inside Birla Temple (Laxmi Narayan Temple)

indica.cards@gmail.com +91-93124 01976

Lord Shiva inside Birla Temple (Laxmi Narayan Temple)

indica.cards@gmail.com +91-93124 01976

Lord Vishnu inside Birla Mandir (Laxmi Narayan Temple)

© Indica Cards • www.mpu.co.in

indica.cards@gmail.com +91-93124 01976

Lord Krishna (Sheesh Mahal) inside Birla Temple (Laxmi Narayan Temple)

to inaugurate the temple. Priests performed the religious ritual of Pran pratishthapna, on Saturday, *Chaitra Krishnapaksha Trayodashi Vikram era* 1995 (18th March, 1939).

The temple is built in the *Nagara* style of architecture interspersed with modern influences. The entire temple is adorned with relief carvings depicting the scenes from mythology. 101 skilled pundits from *Benares*, headed by *Acharya Vishvanath Shastri*, carved the idols of the temple. One can find a number of friezes and artistic sculptures add to the aesthetic beauty of this temple. The highest *Shikara* of the temple above the sanctum sanctorum soars 160 feet high while the ancillary towers reach 116 ft. The temple faces the east and is situated on a high plinth. It leades to a platform from where a few more steps lead to sanctum sanctorum. This chamber is dedicated to *Lord Narayan* and *Goddess Lakshmi*. There are other small shrines dedicated to *Lord Shiva, Lord Ganesha* and *Hanuman*. The holy Vedas are also enshrined in this temple. There is also a shrine dedicated to *Lord Buddha*. The shrine is adorned with fresco paintings depicting his life and work. The icons of the temple are in marble brought from Jaipur. Kota stone from Makarana, Agra, Kota and Jaisalmer were used in the construction of the temple premises. The *Geeta Bhawan* to the north of the temple is dedicated to *Lord Krishna*. The hall is adorned with beautiful paintings depicting scenes from Indian mythology. The temples premises are dotted with miniature rock temples, which are a craze amongst the children. The entire complex, especially the walls and the upper gallery are full of paintings carried out by artists from Jaipur in Rajasthan. An artificial landscape complete with mountains and cascading waterfalls add to the beauty of the temple. The exterior is faced with the white marble and red sandstone typical of Delhi's Mughal architecture. The interior court is overlooked by two-storey verandahs on three sides. The walls of the temple are decorated with various Hindu symbols and quotes from the Gita and the Upanishads.

HINDU SYMBOLS

ॐ OM

OM is the symbol of the idea that God, creator of everything, is infinite, omnipresent, omniscient, omnipotent and imperceptible.

श्री SHREE

Shree is considered to be the symbol of wealth, prosperity, comfort, calm and well-being.

卐 SWASTIKA

Swastika is symbol is most sacred and ancient. At least for more than last 8,000 years, it has been the mark of Aryan (Hindu) civilisation and culture. (Do not confuse it with the Nazi Swastika, which was in reverse form).

This symbol signifies an implied prayer for success, accomplishment and perfection, in every walk of life, under the guidance of the Almighty. It is found not only in India, but in the Buddhist and other foreign countries. For many foreign tourists, this is the place in India where they are confronted with the incongrogous sight of multiple 'swastikas'.

Hinduism is India's indigenous religious and cultural system. Also called *Sanatana Dharma*, "eternal religion", and *Vaidika Dharma*, "religion of the Vedas", Hindusism encompasses a broad spectrum of philosophies ranging from pluralistic theism to absolute monism. Hinduism is not a man-made religion. It was not founded by any single person. Since Hinduism has no founder, anyone who practices Dharma can call himself a Hindu. It is the product of the seers of the Vedas. It was developed from age to age by the teachings of *Avataras, Rishis, Vedas,* the *Upanishads*, the *Gita* and the *Itihasas*. It will exist as long as the world lasts. The Vedas are the foundational scriptures of Hinduism.

SOME QUOTATIONS FROM THE VEDAS

अपध्वान्तमूर्णुहि पूर्धि चक्षुः। (Sam. P.4,- 1-37)

Remove the darkness of the our ignorance and open our eyes to see Truth and Reality.

महे चन त्वामद्रिवः परा शुल्काय देयाम्। (Rig. 8-1-5)

May we ever stick to Thee O Lord! and never desert Thee at any cost!

अस्माकं सन्त्वाशिषः सत्याः। (Yajur.2-10)

May our longings and aspirations, our ideas and ideals, be genuine and generous.

..... Continued on inside back cover

indica.cards@gmail.com +91-93124 01976

Lord Hanuman inside Birla Temple (Laxmi Narayan Temple)

© Indica Cards • www.mpu.co.in

indica.cards@gmail.com +91-93124 01976

Goddesses Durga inside Birla Temple (Laxmi Narayan Temple)

indica.cards@gmail.com +91-93124 01976

Sai Baba is believed to be an incarnation of Lord Shiva and he was regarded as a satguru and an incarnation of Kabir.

indica.cards@gmail.com +91-93124 01976

Left: Shiv Ling (Gupha) inside Birla Temple (Laxmi Narayan Temple) **Right:** Back side view of Birla Temple (Laxmi Narayan Temple)